Too Much Trash!

Dona Herweck Rice

Trash can make **pollution.**

It **harms** water.

It harms land.

It harms air.

It harms birds.

It harms fish.

It harms us.

Do not **pollute**!

Let's Do Science!

What happens to trash when it is buried? Try this!

What to Get

- ❏ bucket of dirt
- ❏ newspaper
- ❏ small shovel
- ❏ trash, such as a can, plastic, and a fruit peel
- ❏ water

What to Do

1 Bury the trash in the bucket. Add water. Mix things with a shovel.

2 Once each week, add more water and mix things up.

3 Wait four or five weeks. Take the trash out of the bucket. Lay it on the newspaper. What has happened to the trash?

Glossary

harms—hurts or damages

pollute—to make dirty in a way that hurts or **damages** things

pollution—trash and dirt that hurts or damages things

Index

Your Turn!

A good way to stop so much trash is to recycle. This means to use something in a new way. Think of a way you can recycle something.